Using Word
Word
IN THE
Classroom

Using Word
IN THE
Classroom

Armand Seguin

Renee M. Eggers

Dusti Howell

With contributions from:

Deanne Howell

Jean Morrow

Jennifer Summerville

CORWIN PRESS, INC.
A Sage Publications Company
Thousand Oaks, California

For information:

Corwin Press, Inc.
A Sage Publications Company
2455 Teller Road
Thousand Oaks, California 91320
E-mail: order@corwinpress.com

Sage Publications Ltd.
6 Bonhill Street
London EC2A 4PU
United Kingdom

Sage Publications India Pvt. Ltd.
M-32 Market
Greater Kailash I
New Delhi 110 048 India

Printed in the United States of America

Library of Congress Cataloging-in-Publication Data

Using Word in the classroom / by Armand Seguin ... [et al.].
    p. cm.
  Includes index.
  ISBN 0-7619-7883-6 (c) — ISBN 0-7619-7884-4 (p)
  1. Microsoft Word. 2. Computer managed instruction.   I. Seguin,
Armand.
 LB1028.46 .U85 2002
 652.5'5369—dc21
                              2001005563
This book is printed on acid-free paper.

02   03   04   05   06   07   7   6   5   4   3   2   1

Acquisitions Editor:	Robb Clouse
Associate Editor:	Kylee Liegl
Editorial Assistant:	Erin Buchanan
Production Editor:	Olivia Weber
Typesetter/Designer:	Larry K. Bramble
Copy Editor:	Carla Freeman
Cover Designer:	Tracy E. Miller

Contents

Preface

Welcome to *Using Word in the Classroom.* This book is for teachers who have access to Microsoft Word and want to do more than just simple word processing. Unlike other books that focus on only one computer platform or version of Microsoft Word, *Using Word in the Classroom* provides instruction for both Windows (Microsoft Word 97 and 2000) and Macintosh (Microsoft Word 98 and 2001).

The authors have designed this book as a step-by-step, how-to book for specific projects and tasks associated with today's classrooms. Steps in each project or task have accompanying images to make it easy for readers to replicate the project or task. In addition, the book contains sections in which the reader can learn more about a particular feature of Microsoft Word, as well as sections containing helpful troubleshooting tips. The various features of Microsoft Word covered in the chapters can then be applied to other Microsoft Word-based projects designed by teachers.

Acknowledgments

We would like to extend our sincere appreciation to our colleagues in the field and in the classroom who read this text, tested our ideas, and provided feedback and support during the editorial process. The following reviewers are gratefully acknowledged:

Gregg Elder
Teacher-Librarian, Technical Chair
Evergreen Middle School
Everett, WA

Robin Van Heyningenke West
Teacher
White River High School
Buckley, WA

Ken Martin
Coordinator of Curriculum and Instruction
University of Cincinnati
College of Education
Cincinnati, OH

Blake West
District Coordinating Teacher for
     Technology
Blue Valley Schools
Overland Park, KS

Kristen L. Blake
Teacher
La Habra High School
La Habra, CA

Joe Meersman
Teacher
Toppenish High School
Toppenish, WA

Richard J. Marchesani
Assistant Professor of Education
Elmira College
Elmira, NY

Eric Alm
Teacher
Jenkins High School
Chewelah, WA

Katherine Avila
Teacher
Tewksbury Memorial High School
Tewksbury, MA

Ellen Thompson
Teacher
Horizon Elementary School
Madison, AL

Fred MacDonald
Program Officer
Standards of Practice and Education
Ontario College of Teachers
Toronto, Canada

Tawn Rundle
Teacher/Elementary Technology
   Coordinator
Laverne Public Schools
Laverne, OR

Note: All screen shots are reprinted
by permission of Microsoft Corporation.

About the Authors

Armand Seguin is Associate Professor and Chair of the Department of Instructional Design and Technology at Emporia State University. He is keenly interested in the impact of technology on the classroom teacher and was an early adopter of the Apple IIe. Other interests include teaching via distance learning. He initiated one of the first on-line courses in the country when he delivered Electronic Mail for Educators via the Alaska Computer Network in 1986. He has delivered many professional presentations and is active in the Association for Teacher Educators; he chaired its Commission on Utilizing Technology in Educational Reform. He holds membership in the Association for Educational Communications & Technology, the Society for Information Technology in Education, and the Mid-America Association for Computers in Education. He holds an EdD from Arizona State University, a master's degree from Indiana State University, and a bachelor's degree from St. Cloud State University. He has taught at Dakota State University, University of Alaska Southeast, Jackson State University, and West Virginia State College.

He was born and raised in Minneapolis, Minnesota, and likes water, including the ocean. He owned and operated a commercial fishing boat in Southeast Alaska for 15 years. He is married to Cynthia Seguin, who is also a professor of education at Emporia State University. His son, Mathew, lives in Juneau, Alaska.

Renee M. Eggers is Assistant Professor at Youngstown State University, where she teaches undergraduate and graduate courses in educational technology. She is the author of several articles dealing with use and integration of technology in educational situations. In addition to being a member of the Technology Commission for the Association of Teacher Educators, she is a member of Ohio's Statewide Technology Framework Committee.

Dusti D. Howell earned a PhD in curriculum and instruction, with an emphasis in educational communications and technology, and a PhD minor in educational psychology from the University of Wisconsin–

Madison. He is currently teaching at Emporia State University in the Instructional Design and Technology Department. His expertise includes high-tech study skills and digital learning strategies, multimedia, and video production. He teaches on-line courses including, "Powerful Presentations in PowerPoint" and "Fundamental 4Mat Training." He has taught every grade level from first grade through graduate school. He is currently president of the local chapter of Phi Delta Kappa.

Deanne K. Howell teaches professional development courses for university faculty and staff. She conducts professional development workshops, on-line courses, and classes for Emporia State University. Deanne holds a master's degree in science education from the University of Wisconsin–Madison. She has taught in public, private, and international schools.

Jean Morrow, OSM, EdD, has 40 years of classroom teaching experience at all levels, from first grade through university. Jean has been a member of Servants of Mary since 1958. She earned a master's degree in mathematics education from the University of Detroit and a doctorate in instructional design and technology from Boston University. Co-author of two books on mathematics instruction, she is a frequent speaker at state and national meetings. Her favorite theme for those talks is the integration of technology and problem solving. Most recently, Jean has been teaching classes over the Internet for Emporia State University in Emporia, Kansas. She serves on the Board of Examiners for the National Council for the Accreditation of Teacher Education. In 1998, she was given the Distinguished Clinician Award in Teacher Education by the Association of Teacher Educators.

Jennifer Summerville is Assistant Professor of Instructional Design and Technology at Emporia State University. She received a master's degree in computer education and cognitive systems from the University of North Texas and a PhD in educational technology, with an emphasis in distance education, instructional design, and interactive multimedia design, from the University of Northern Colorado. She specializes in instructional design, distance education, and instructional media design. Her research interests include integration of technology in the K-12 classroom, learner-centered issues in distance education, and cognitive and personality issues in the design and development of instruction.

1

Introduction to Microsoft® Word

Welcome to the world of Microsoft Word. As an educator, you have chosen to use the most popular word processing program in the world. And although we will be dealing only with Word, it is often sold in a package called Microsoft Office Suite, with versions 97 and 2000 for computers running Microsoft Windows as the operating system, and Office 98 and 2001 for computers using Apple's Macintosh Operating System. In addition to Word, the other programs in the standard package include Excel, a spreadsheet; PowerPoint, a presentation program; and Outlook Express, a program used for electronic mail. Microsoft Word has come out in several versions; in this book, we address Word 97 and 2000 for Windows, and Word 98 and 2001 for the Macintosh.

One important difference between the Macintosh and Windows version is the use of keyboard shortcuts. Windows uses the **Ctrl** key, the equivalent of the **Command** key on the Macintosh. While holding down **Ctrl** or **Command⌘,** press down on a particular key (e.g., "S" for "Save") to execute a task. The directions for this shortcut look like this: **Ctrl/⌘+ S**

Helpful Features of This Book

✔**Troubleshooting Tip:** Includes possible problems you may encounter with alternative methods for performing the task. Time-saving tips will also be found here.

Learn More: Experiment and try out the suggested ideas to become more proficient with Word.

Most of the directions in this book work for all four versions. When there are differences, look for the following:

WIN or WINDOWS	Windows versions 97 and 2000 only
MAC or MACINTOSH	Macintosh versions 98 and 2001 only
WIN 97	Windows version 97 only
WIN 00	Windows 2000 only
MAC 98	Macintosh version 98 only
MAC 01	Macintosh version 2001 only

What Version of Word Am I Using?

To find out exactly which version you are using on the Windows platform, you will need to have already started Word. Windows users should click on **Help** on the **Menubar** and then click on **About Microsoft Word.** An information box will pop up, similar to the one pictured.

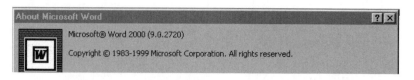

Figure 1.1   About Microsoft Word

MACINTOSH

Macintosh users can obtain similar information by clicking on the **Apple Menu** (top left of screen) and selecting **About Microsoft Word.**

Similarity Between Versions

The good news is that for regular users of word processing, there are only minor differences between any of these versions: If you learn on one, you can easily transfer this knowledge to any other package. Furthermore, many of the commands are identical or very similar in Excel, PowerPoint, and many other programs. Thus, familiarity with word processing, the most popular computer task of all, and learning Microsoft Word will also quickly enable the beginner to use other programs running in the Windows operating system.

Uses and Features

Microsoft Word has numerous uses in the classroom. For example:

▶ Write letters to students, parents, colleagues, and administrators.

▶ Create lesson plans, including a "template" that can be used over and over.

▶ Produce newsletters, either keeping them simple or using Word's features to rival a dedicated publishing program. The letters and newsletters can include graphics as well as multiple typefaces and sizes.

In addition, it is easy to use Word to make relatively simple Web pages. If your software is set up for it, you can also use Word to compose electronic mail messages. As you will find out, Microsoft Word is a very versatile tool for both teachers and students.

Starting Word

WINDOWS

There are several ways to start, or open, Microsoft Word. The most common way is to put your cursor on the **Start** button, on the far left of the toolbar at the bottom of the screen. Hold down the left mouse button and the **Start window** will pop up. Continue holding the button down while scrolling up to the **Programs folder** to open the menu of pro-

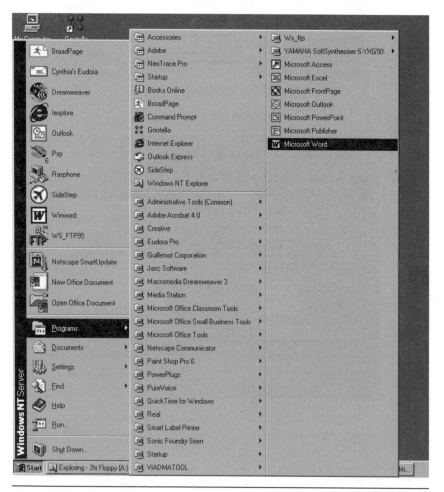

Figure 1.2   Open Word

grams on your computer. Double-click on **Microsoft Word** to open/launch the application program.

An alternative way to start the program is to find the **Office Shortcut Bar** that may be available on your desktop. If the shortcut bar is available, simply click on the **Word** icon and the program will open.

MACINTOSH

To open Microsoft Word on the Apple Macintosh, click on the **Apple Menu** icon located at the top left of the screen to bring down the menu. Go down to **Recent Applications** and click on Microsoft Word to open up the application (this only works if it was used recently). Alternatively, double-click the **Hard Drive** icon, often labeled **Macintosh HD,** at the top right of the screen; this brings up the Macintosh Hard Drive window, which indicates all of the programs and documents stored on your computer's hard drive.

1. Double-click on the **Microsoft Office folder.**
   The Microsoft Office window will appear.

2. Double-click on the **Microsoft Word icon.**

ALL VERSIONS

Most screens will open as white, but some can open as gray (depending on previous use), and selected features will not be shown until you have actually opened a document. The top of the screen shows the **Menubar, Standard Toolbar,** and **Formatting Bar.** Microsoft Word is highly customizable, and your screen may show different items at the top. When Word is first installed, all settings are set to "default," which is the "standard" or most common setting. However, individual users may have changed features such as the typeface, type size, page layout, or which toolbars to view. To set Word to look like the screens in this book, put the cursor on **View** on the **Menubar** and scroll down to **Toolbars**.

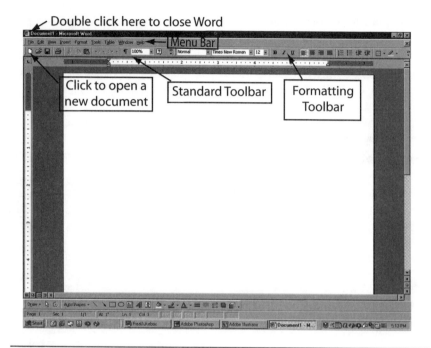

Figure 1.3 Opening Screen

Be sure to have only **Standard** and **Formatting** checked. Word offers several options to open a file, but the "quick start" (use this step only if your screen opened as gray) is to put the cursor on the **New Blank Document** icon on the far left of the toolbar, directly under **File,** and click the left mouse button. This opens a "clean" new page, called a "document" in Word.

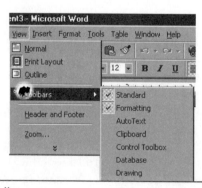

Figure 1.4 Toolbars

Learn More: The most frequently used toolbar items are the **New Blank Document, Open, Save,** and **Print** icons. These functions are all on the left side of the toolbar.

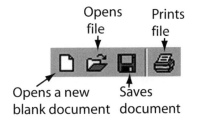

Opens file

Prints file

Opens a new blank document

Saves document

Click on to shrink/enlarge the window

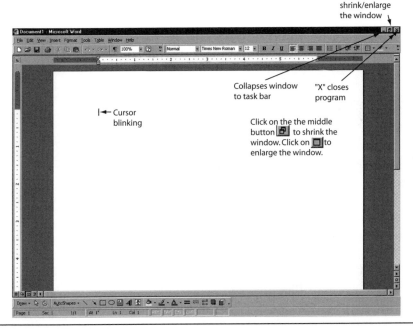

Collapses window to task bar

"X" closes program

Cursor blinking

Click on the the middle button to shrink the window. Click on to enlarge the window.

Figure 1.5 Upper Right

WINDOWS

The three controls in the upper right corner should be addressed now because they control the size and placement of the "window."

The document window can open in varying sizes, or even off to one side of the screen, and may need to be resized. Clicking on the middle icon, a "full window," will make the active window full screen.

Clicking on the middle icon, shown as "overlapping windows," makes the window less than full screen and also means you can use the Microsoft Windows "drag" feature to create a window of any size.

The left icon, or "bar," will collapse the screen into the taskbar at the bottom of your desktop. The far-right **X** will close the window, which also closes Microsoft Word.

 Learn More: Experiment with the Windows "drag" feature. Put the cursor in any corner of the window (only bottom right in **MAC)** until it becomes an angled arrow. By touching the mouse button, you can "drag" the window to any size.

MACINTOSH

The top row of the work area window is called the **Title Bar.** The **Close Box** on the far left of this bar closes the window when clicked. (Note: This does not close Word. It is still open when the **Application menu** in the top right corner of the screen is selected.) Two other buttons are located on the far right side of the title bar. The first is the **Zoom Box,** which changes the size of the window when clicked. The **Collapse Box** in the far right corner collapses the window but leaves the title bar open on the screen.

Help!

Help may be only a mouse click away! You'll be pleased to know that Word has provided several major ways to get help. First, Word includes the "Office Assistant." The paper clip icon can show up nearly anywhere on your window. In addition, it will occasionally "wink" at you and make faces! The Office Assistant is active by default.

1. Click on the Office Assistant and a screen will appear, asking, "What would you like to do?"

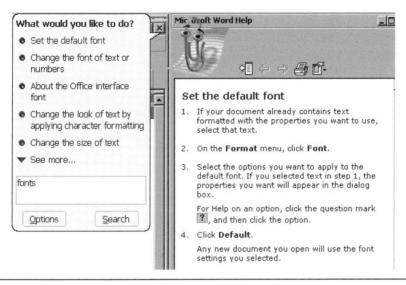

Figure 1.6 Font Question

2. Type in "fonts," then **Enter/Return,** and the bulleted items will focus on font items.

3. Selecting "Set the default font" from the list of topics brings up an answer window on the right side of the screen.

   MAC 01: Click on "See more ..." to view this option.

   MAC: The Mac Assistant looks like a "friendly computer." By clicking on it, you will be able to key in a question.

Word has thousands of topics available, and many answers include several suggestions and links to "additional resources."

Microsoft Word also lets you "Hide the Office Assistant." This option is available by **Right-clicking (MAC: Ctrl + Click)** on the Office Assistant and selecting "Hide" or "Hide Assistant" from the drop-down menu. Select **Options** and click on the "Use the Office Assistant" box to turn off the assistant.

When you select **Help > Microsoft Word Help**, you will see a different help screen. In the screen following, we keyed in "table" as a keyword on the **Index** tab.

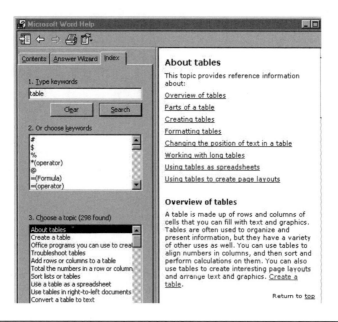

Figure 1.7   "Help" Menu

MAC 98:   The help screens look very similar to version 2001.

Figure 1.8   Mac "Help" Screen

Help With Spelling

Finally, one of the most popular features is help with spelling! You can misspell a word, and Microsoft Word will automatically underline the word with a red squiggly line.

wrd

In addition, it will "automatically correct" the spelling of most words while you are keying them in to the screen! More on using the "spell checker" later in the book.

We have a new blank document, and the next chapter will show how to create a lesson plan and save it for future use.

Quick Review

▶ **What Version of Word Am I Using?**

WIN: Help > About Microsoft Word

MAC: Apple > About Microsoft Word

▶ **Launching Word:**

WIN: Start > Programs > Word

MAC: Double-click on Hard Drive icon, double-click on MS Office folder, double-click on Word

▶ **Standard Toolbars Used:**

View >Toolbars and select Standard and Formatting

▶ **Common Tools Used:**

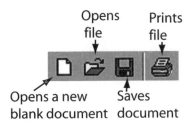

Opens file

Prints file

Opens a new blank document

Saves document

► **Help Options/Office Assistant:**

Help > Microsoft Word Help brings up the "Help" contents

Click on Office Assistant, type in the topic or question, Enter/Return, click on the topic to learn more

► **Turn off Assistant:**

WIN: Right-click on Hide

MAC: Ctrl + click on Hide

► **Other Information:**

WINDOWS Ctrl key = MACINTOSH Command key

Creating Lesson Plans and Forms

---

*T*his chapter will include developing several items frequently needed in the typical classroom: lesson plans and hall passes. The user will also be introduced to Word features, such as creating templates, "copying and pasting," numbering, and how to print. Users will also learn how to preview a document prior to printing.

Creating a Lesson Plan

For the first word processing document in this chapter, we will create an outline for a lesson plan and save the document. The lesson plan document will then be changed to a "template" so that it can easily be used again and again. In Chapter 7, we will convert the lesson plan document to a Web page.

There is a template for all documents. This determines several settings, including the font and paper sizes; a template can also contain prespecified information, as in a "blank lesson plan" or a personalized "letterhead."

1. **Open Microsoft Word** and key in the following information:

"Teacher," and press the **Tab** key three times

Type your name, your school, and **Enter/ Return** twice

"Subject Area," then **Enter/Return** twice

"Unit Title," **Enter/Return** twice

"Lesson Title," **Enter/ Return** twice

"Objectives," **Enter/Return** twice

"Needd Materials," **Enter/ Return** six times

"Procedure," **Enter/Return** fourteen times

"Additional Comments"

2. **Spell checking**. Note the squiggly line beneath the word "Needd." Word has an automatic spell checker that alerts you to possible typographical errors or misspellings. **Right-click** (**MAC: Ctrl + click**) on the word "Needd" to view suggested replacements for the word. Click on the correct spelling, "Needed."

✔ **Troubleshooting Tip:** The spell checker's dictionary is limited. Words underlined in red are not necessarily misspelled. If in doubt, consult a standard dictionary.

3. Adjust the spaces between the categories as needed, especially "Objectives" and "Procedure," by clicking **Enter/Return**, but keep this document to one page. When the bottom of the page is reached, a dotted line runs across the screen with "Page Break" in the middle, or the screen will "jump" to a new page.

4. If necessary, use the keyboard's **Backspace** (often a left-hand arrow) or **Delete** keys to "adjust the spacing" and eliminate a page break (an extra blank line or two would cause a second sheet to print blank).

 Learn More: There are times when you want to purposely insert a page break into a document. Two examples: when using a title page or when starting a new chapter.

Saving a Document

1. Click on the **Save** button located on the left side of the toolbar.

    For a document that has NOT been named, the following screen(s) comes up (Figure 2.1 for Windows; Figures 2.2 and 2.3 for Macs).

2. Note the file name shown toward the bottom. Word may suggest using the name "Teacher," or "Teacher" along with your name, because these are the first words typed in the document.

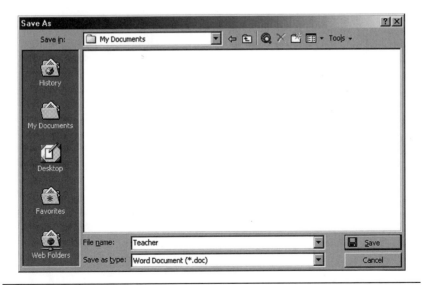

Figure 2.1   Save As "Teacher"

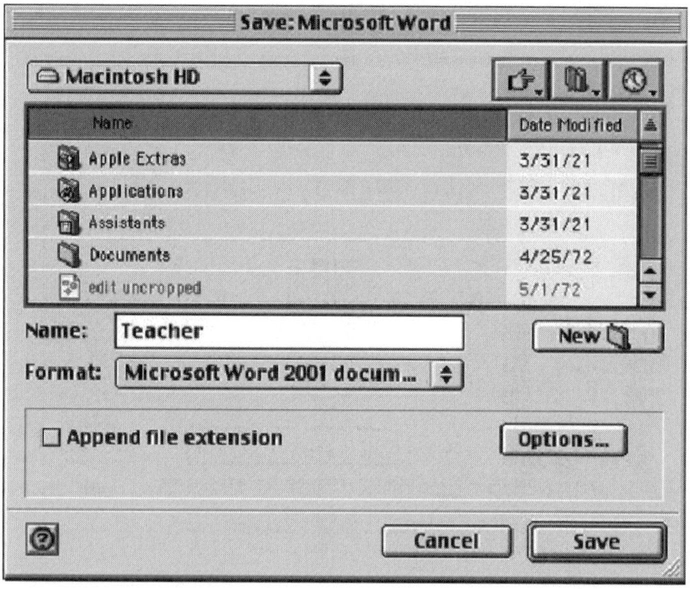

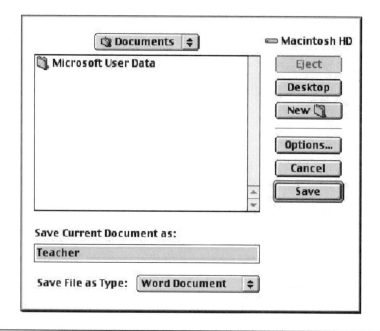

Figure 2.2 Mac 2001, Save As "Teacher"

Figure 2.3 Mac 98, Save As "Teacher"

3. Replace the selected text with "**Lesson Plan**." Note that as soon the "L" in "Lesson Plan" is touched, "Teacher" is replaced by the new name.

4. Use the navigation window at the top of the dialog box only if you wish to save the document to a different location on your hard drive.

   WIN: In the "Save As" dialog box, use the default setting, "My Documents" in the C: drive.

   MAC: Save onto the hard drive (often titled **Macintosh HD**). If the hard drive is not found in the drop-down box, choose "Desktop," then locate and double-click on the hard drive icon in the main window.

5. Press the **Save** button in the dialog box or press **Enter/Return**.

Learn More: File names can be upper- and/or lowercase and can be very long. Many people use lowercase letters simply because it is easier. On the Macintosh, file names are limited to 31 characters.

Troubleshooting Tip: It is very important to note WHERE on the hard disk files are saved. In this example, "Lesson Plan" was saved to the default folder, "My Documents." Although this may sound quite simple, it is very common for new users to "lose" their files. Thus, it is strongly encouraged that files be saved to the same location.

Formatting Text, Numbering, and Using "Save As Template"

The document is complete and has been saved as a document, but it is still "open." We will now change it to a template, but first we will add automatic "Numbering" to "Objectives" and then boldface the main topics before saving it. To do this,

1. Go to the document and place the cursor one line below "Objectives."

2. Go to **Format > Bullets and Numbering**.

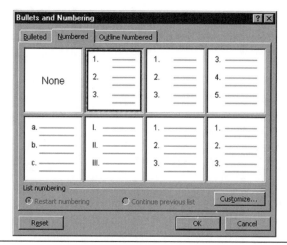

Figure 2.4   Bullets and Numbering

3. From the dialog box, select **Numbered** then the **1. 2. 3.** format. The number **1** will be inserted, and the succeeding number will be automatically inserted whenever you enter an objective and then tap the **Enter/Return** key.

4. Next, go to **Edit > Select All.** All the text on the screen is highlighted.

5. Select the **Bold** button on the **Formatting Toolbar**.

6. Click on the document outside of the highlighted area. The typeface becomes bold or darker, and it is slightly larger.

7. Click on **File > Save As**. Find "Save As Type" near the bottom (**MAC 01:** find "Format" and **MAC 98**: "Save File As Type"), click on the "down" arrow key and select "Document Template."

8. Click on the **Save** button in the dialog box.

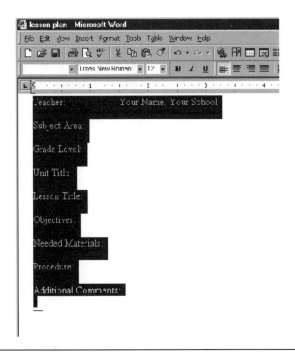

Figure 2.5   Select All

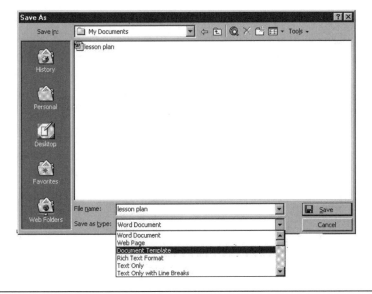

Figure 2.6   Save As Template

"Document Templates" are different from "Documents" and are stored in a different folder called "Templates" or "My Templates."

The templates "show up" when you choose **File > New (MAC 01: File > Project Gallery)** and select "My Templates" under "Categories."

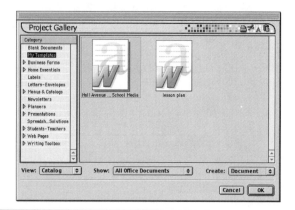

Figure 2.7   Macintosh Project Gallery

Recall that when you simply want to open a "New" standard document, you need only click on the **New Blank Document** button on the far left.

✔ **Troubleshooting Tip:** Microsoft Word documents in Windows are stored as files, with a file name plus the extension. The extension for any regular document is ".doc." Thus, "Lesson Plan" is automatically stored as "Lesson Plan.doc." When we saved "Lesson Plan" as a document template, it was automatically assigned the "dot" extension for "document template." Note that we now have two documents with the same title but with different extensions. Thus, when we go to "open" files that are documents, we will not normally be able to see the names of "document templates." And when we "open" templates, we will not see documents.

Opening a Template and Saving With New Title

This section will show you how to open the template and then resave it with a name specific to a class.

1. Click on **File > New > Lesson Plan** in the **General** tab and select **OK**.

>   **MAC 01:**   **File > New Project Gallery**. Select "My Templates" from the "Categories" window. Then select "Lesson Plan" and click **OK**.

✔ **Troubleshooting Tip:** If **New** is not an option under **File**, double-click on **File**. Note, the **New Document** button does not bring up the template options.

>   **WIN 00:**   Note that the first three templates, "Blank Document," "Web Page," and "E-Mail Message" are preinstalled by Microsoft Word.

>   **WIN 97 & MAC 98:**   Only the "Blank Document" is preinstalled.

>   **MAC 01:**   Nothing is preinstalled in the "My Templates" folder.
>
>   There are also many other templates found under the other tabs or categories, and users are encouraged to explore them.

2. **File > Save As.** Microsoft Word will suggest the file name of "Teacher" because this is the first word in the document. However, the user should assign a title that will coincide with the lesson plan that you will place "into" the template. For this example, we will title it "Language Arts 1."

3. "Teacher" will be highlighted, and when you begin to input "Language Arts 1," the name "Teacher" is replaced. Select **Save**.

4. Select **File > Close.**

You will now have two templates: one generic "Lesson Plan" with no class title and a second example with the title "Language Arts 1."

You may wish to use your own class titles so these templates are ready for your personal use.

Creating a Form

There are many types of forms that are useful for classroom teachers, including those for field trips, disciplinary action, sporting events, and hall passes. This example will create a hall pass, and because it will be small, we will put two forms on one page.

1. Open a new blank document using the **New** button on the far left of the **Toolbar Menu.**

2. Enter a heading of the school name and/or location (e.g., "Anyplace Middle School, Middlecity, Missouri"). **Enter/Return** twice and add "Hall Pass."

3. Highlight school name, city, and "Hall Pass" by holding down the mouse button and dragging the cursor over the headings.

4. Boldface the font, change it to 14 pt., and center the heading. All of these features are on the **Formatting Toolbar.** Click on the **bold** button, change the number next to the the bold button by clicking on the "down" arrow and selecting 14 for the font size. Next, select the **Center Alignment** button.

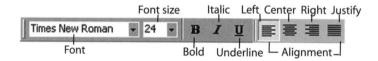

5. Click off of the text to view the formatting changes.

6. Add three blank lines after "Hall Pass" with **Enter/Return.**

7. Click on **Table > Insert Table**. In the "Insert Table" dialog box, select "2 columns" and "2 rows" by clicking on the "up" or "down" arrows, then **OK.** Click off of the table to view the changes.

8. Enter "Student's Name:" "Date:" and "Time:" in the table as shown.

Student's Name:	
Date:	Time:

9. Highlight the table. Select the **Align Left** button.

10. Add one blank line above each term in the table by placing the cursor at the beginning of each line (before "S," "D," and "T") and tap **Enter/Return** for each.

Student's Name:	
Date:	Time:

11. Put the cursor below the info boxes (**Name, Date** and **Time** table) and add three blank lines by tapping **Enter/Return** three times. Change the alignment to the right by clicking on the **Align Right** button.

12. Input "Sincerely" and press **Enter/Return** twice.

13. Add the line for a signature by using the **Underline** key. Hold the **Shift** key and touch the **Underline** key about 30 times (note that the line comes from the right and the underline is added to the left). Press **Enter/Return**.

✔ **Troubleshooting Tip:** If "AutoFormat" puts a bold line across the entire screen, press **Edit > Undo** or click the **Undo** button.

14. Input teacher's name under the line.

15. Save the document as "Hall Pass."

Copy and Paste

Because the "Hall Pass" is a relatively small document, we'll use the "Copy and Paste" function to create a duplicate and allow for the printing of two passes on one sheet of paper.

The preceding document was saved but not closed, so it will still be the active window. It will look like this:

Anyplace Middle School, Middlecity, Missouri

HALL PASS

Student's Name:	
Date:	**Time:**

Sincerely,
(teacher's name)

---

1. Highlight the full document by selecting **Edit > Select All.**

2. Click on the **Copy** button, on the **Standard Toolbar** (it is "grayed out" and unavailable until text or graphics are highlighted), then click off of the text.

 Learn More: Both in Windows and on the Macintosh, items that are "copied" (or "cut") are placed into a temporary file called the "clipboard." Whatever is copied replaces anything that was previously in the clipboard.

3. Move the cursor four lines below the line with "Teacher's Name" and paste "Hall Pass" onto the page.

4. **Save** the document.

Note: The document was previously named "Hall Pass," and by "saving," we have replaced the previous title with the reworked document that actually contains *two* hall passes.

Previewing a Document

Any document can be "previewed" prior to printing to see how it will fit onto the paper. This "view" feature can allow the user to make adjustments to the formatting. For example, if the user had too few spaces or too many, the hall passes would not be identical or one pass might be partially onto a second page.

1. Click on **File > Print Preview**.

✔️ **Troubleshooting Tip:** If you do not see "Print Preview" from the drop-down menu, double-click on **File** to get the full list of file options.

2. If the document is just over one page, click on the **Shrink To Fit** button.

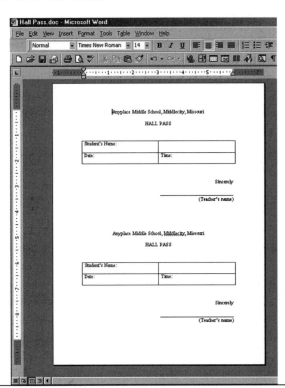

Figure 2.8   Hall Passes

3. To return to the regular view, go to **View > Normal**.

Printing a Document

Microsoft Word offers several choices for printing a document. Printing is a straightforward procedure when the printer has been installed and is turned on. The simplest way is to select the **Print** button from the toolbar.

Make sure the printer is turned on; then, if you have closed "Hall Pass," open it back up and click on the print button. The document is sent to the printer, but you don't see anything different on the screen. You should have printed two hall passes on a document of a single page. If you want a second page with two additional hall passes, simply click on the print button one more time. Using the print button would print all of the pages of your document.

Microsoft Word offers additional printing features by selecting **File > Print**.

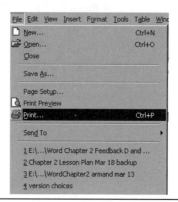

Figure 2.9   File Print

A "print window" will appear that offers several choices. Typically, only one printer will be available, and it is shown by **Name.** In the **Page Range** area, you could choose to print "All" pages, the "Current Page," or a range of pages, say "5-10." You can also select how many copies you want under **Copies.** Click on the "up" arrow to increase the number.

MAC: The print choices are also available, but selecting a printer is from a different menu.

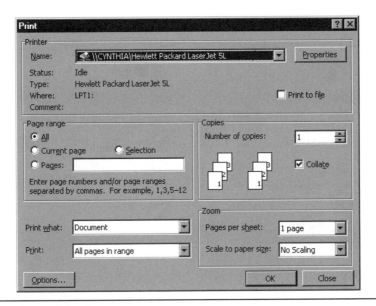

Figure 2.10 Print Box

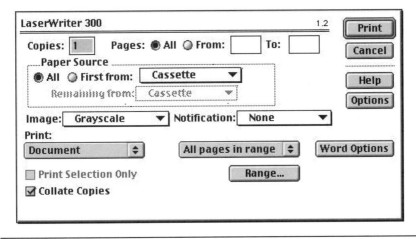

Figure 2.11 Mac Print Box

✔ **Troubleshooting Tip:** Save your documents before printing. If your computer sends a document to the printer and the printer is not turned on, or it becomes jammed, the computer may "freeze." Saving your document first will prevent you from loosing any files if you have to reboot the computer.

Quick Review

▶ **Spell Check:**

Right-click (**MAC:** Ctrl + click) on the misspelled word and select the correct spelling from the drop-down menu.

▶ **Save a Document:**

Save button > Name the document > Find the location to save in the navigation window at the top > Press Save button.

▶ **Save a Template:**

File > Save As. In the Save As Type (MAC: "Format") window select Document Template > Save button.

▶ **Open a Template:**

File > New. Choose a template from the General tab.

▶ **Select All Text:**

Edit > Select All.

▶ **Formatting Text Commands:**

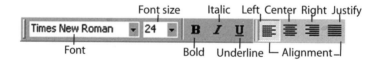

▶ **Insert a Table:**

Table > Insert Table.

▶ **Cut, Copy, and Paste Commands:**

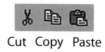

Cut Copy Paste

▶ **Previewing a Document:**

File > Print Preview. Use the Shrink To Fit button to fit text on one page.

▶ **Printing a Document:**

Print button or by File > Print and menu choices.

Creating Stationery

With Microsoft Word, stationery for any purpose can easily be created from a blank document. As part of the stationery creation process, this chapter examines the use of clip art, margins, a text box, lines, and a template that uses the document protection feature.

Beginning the Letterhead: Changing Margins

1. With a blank document opened in Microsoft Word, set the margins for the stationery. To do this, select **File > Page Setup (MAC: Format > Document)**.

2. When the dialog box appears, click on the **Margins** tab and change all four margins to **0.7"** by clicking on the "down" arrow to the right of each margin until **0.7"** appears. Click the **OK** button.

3. Make sure the **Left Alignment** button on the toolbar is selected. A blinking cursor is now next to the left margin.

4. Hit **Enter/Return** twice, then tap the "up" arrow twice to move the cursor back to the top.

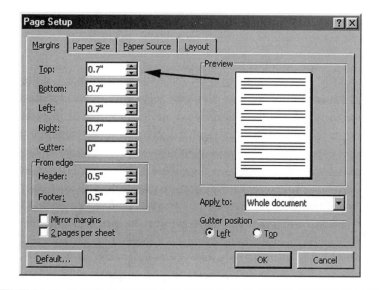

Figure 3.1   Changing Margins

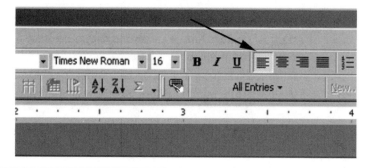

Figure 3.2   Left Alignment Button

Adding Clip Art

1. To add the clip art to the stationery, go to the **Menubar** and click on **Insert > Picture > Clip Art.** A "Clip Art" dialog box appears.

 Learn More: If the desired graphic is stored on the hard drive or on a disk, click on **Insert > Picture > From File** to locate the graphic.

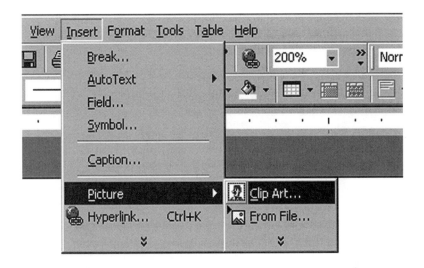

Figure 3.3   Inserting Clip Art

 Learn More: There are two ways to find desired clip art. The first way is the search for all graphics that are related to a keyword that has been entered into the box to the right of the "Search" window. (**MAC 98**: Click on the **Find** button if no search window is available.) A second way of searching for a suitable graphic is to click on the appropriate category. Once a category is selected by clicking on it, graphics related to that category appear.

2. For this example, click on the "Academic" category. (**MAC**: Make sure the **Clip Art** tab is selected.)

3. Select the graphic of an owl reading a book or related graphic.

    MAC: Select any choice of graphic; clips vary in Microsoft Clip Gallery. Double-click on your choice to place it in the document.

    WIN: A "Call Box" appears that contains four buttons. Click the first button, which is the **Insert Clip** button.

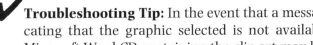 **Troubleshooting Tip:** In the event that a message appears indicating that the graphic selected is not available, the original Microsoft Word CD containing the clip art may have to be placed into the computer's CD drive.

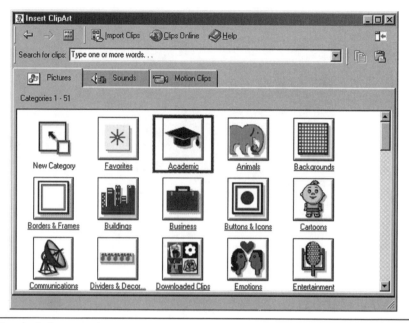

Figure 3.4   Windows 2000 "Clip Art" Dialog Box

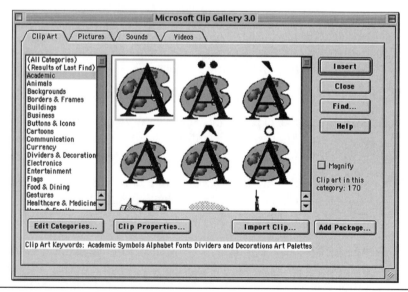

Figure 3.5   Macintosh 98 Clip Gallery Dialog Box

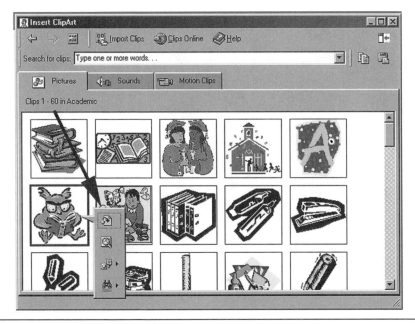

Figure 3.6   Selecting Clip Art

4. The selected graphic now appears on the document. However, the graphic may need to be resized. To resize the graphic, select it by clicking on the graphic. Eight small boxes will appear around the graphic. In the example, the resized graphic is approximately 1 inch by 1.5 inches.

Troubleshooting Tip: If the "Clip Art" dialog box does not disappear at this point, click on the **Close** button at the top corner of the title bar.

5. Press down on the small box located in the lower right corner of the graphic. With the mouse button still held down, drag the mouse in the appropriate diagonal direction until it is the appropriate size. Release the mouse button.

Learn More: To make the graphic smaller, drag the mouse diagonally toward the center of the graphic. To make the graphic larger, drag the mouse diagonally away from the center of the graphic.

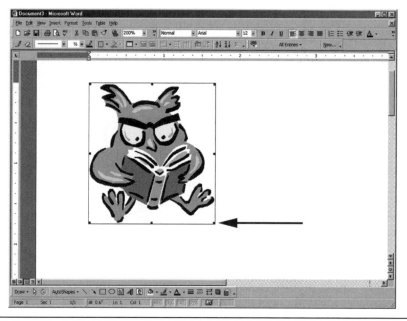

Figure 3.7   Resizing Clip Art

6. Click in the blank area of the document to deselect the graphic. The small boxes surrounding the graphic disappear. (**WIN 97**: Press the **Enter** key on the computer's keyboard once.)

Adding a Text Box

With the graphic added, the next step in creating stationery is to add the address information to be placed next to the graphic. Go to the **Drawing Toolbar** and click on the **Text Box** button.

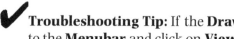 **Troubleshooting Tip:** If the **Drawing Toolbar** is not visible, go to the **Menubar** and click on **View > Toolbars > Drawing.**

1. The cursor now looks like a "plus" sign. Place the cursor near but slightly away from the top right corner of the graphic.

2. Press and hold the mouse down while dragging the mouse diagonally toward the right margin. Make sure the bottom of the text box is no lower than the bottom of the graphic next to the text box.

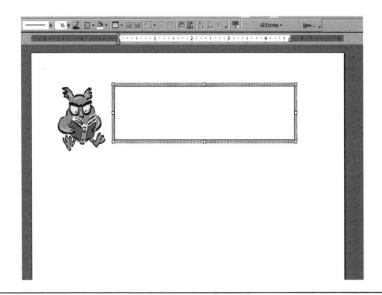

Figure 3.8   Text Box

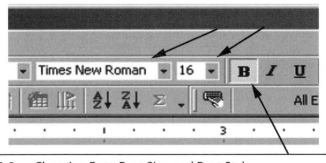

Figure 3.9   Choosing Font, Font Size, and Font Style

3. To add the address information to the text box, go to the toolbar
    and select the desired font, font size, and font style. For this
    example, choose **Times New Roman** as the font, choose a font
    size of **16**, and choose **B** (or Bold) for the font style.

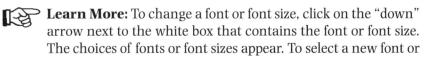 **Learn More:** To change a font or font size, click on the "down"
arrow next to the white box that contains the font or font size.
The choices of fonts or font sizes appear. To select a new font or
font size from the choices available, simply click on the desired
font or font size.

Learn More: Once a document has been created, a font can be changed. Simply highlight the words for which the font change is desired, go to the white box on the toolbar that contains the font names, click on the "down" arrow, and then click on the desired font.

4. At this point, the address can now be placed inside the text box. For this example, do the following:

   • Input "Hall Avenue High School Media Center" and **Enter/ Return**

   • Input "534 Hall Avenue" and **Enter/Return**

   • Input "Anycity, FL 33xxx" and **Enter/Return**

   • Input "mediacenter@hallhigh.k12.us.edu."

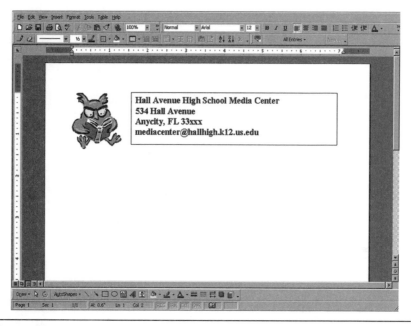

Figure 3.10 Text Box

5. The information has been entered inside the text box so the border of the text box can now be made invisible by placing the cursor on top of the border. When the cursor turns into a "plus" sign with arrows at each end, double-click on the border to bring up the "Format Text Box" dialog box.

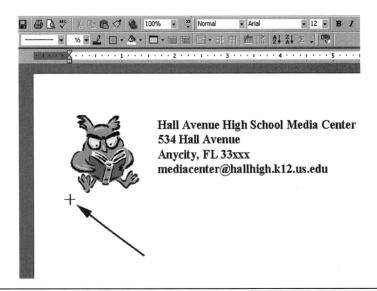

Hall Avenue High School Media Center
534 Hall Avenue
Anycity, FL 33xxx
mediacenter@hallhigh.k12.us.edu

Figure 3.11 Line Cursor

6. Click on the **Colors and Lines** tab. In the "Line" area, click on the "down" arrow to the right of the box next to "Color."

7. At this point, a color palette appears. Click on "No Line," then **OK**.

8. Click in the blank area below the text box to see what the stationery looks like without the border.

Inserting a Line

1. To add a line that separates the top of the stationery from the rest of the stationery, go to the **Drawing Toolbar** and click on the **Line** button. (See Figure 3.12.)

2. With the cursor now looking like a "plus" sign, go to the area just below the graphic and hold the mouse button down while dragging the cursor toward the right margin. (See Figure 3.13.)

Troubleshooting Tip: In the event of difficulty in attempting to draw a straight line, simply press and hold the **Shift** key while holding down the mouse button. The line straightens.

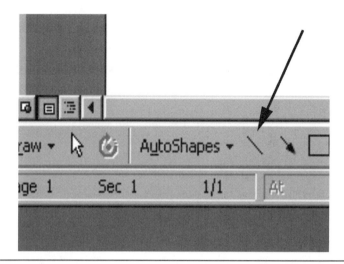

Figure 3.12   Line Style Button

Hall Avenue High School Media Center
534 Hall Avenue
Anycity, FL 33xxx
mediacenter@hallhigh.k12.us.edu

Figure 3.13   Active Line

3. When the line appears horizontal, release the mouse button. If the **Shift** key has been pressed, release it.

4. To alter the appearance of the line in some way, click on the line to make it active. When the line is active, a small white box appears at either end of the line.

5. Click on the **Line Style** button on the **Drawing Toolbar.** The **Line Style** menu now appears.

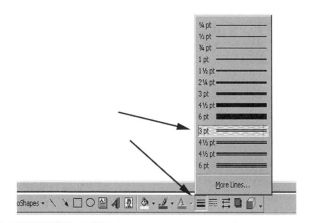

Figure 3.14 Changing Line Style

6. To select a new line style, click on the desired line style. For this example, click on **3 pt.**, which looks like parallel lines. The line has now changed from the single line to two parallel lines.

Protecting the Letterhead

To make sure that newly created stationery is not altered accidentally or on purpose, the stationery can be "password protected." When a document or part of a document is password protected, no one can make any changes to the words, font, or graphic in the protected part of the document unless the person has the special password that will enable desired changes to be made.

1. To protect this document, click the cursor in the middle of the document. The cursor should begin blinking in the left margin below the line.

2. Insert a "Continuous Section Break." Go to **Insert > Break.** In the "Break" dialog box, click inside the circle to the left of **Continuous,** then press **OK.**

   MAC 01: Go to **Insert > Break > Section Break (Continuous)** or **Insert > Section Break**.

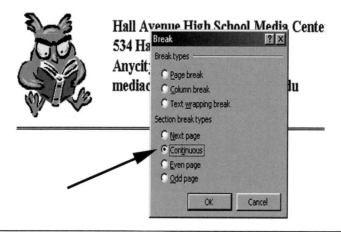

Figure 3.15   Inserting a Section Break

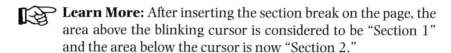

✔**Troubleshooting Tip:** If you are working on a Mac and the cursor jumps to page 2, select **Format > Section**. In the "Section" dialog box, select the "up" or "down" arrow in the "Section Start" window and select "Continuous." Select **OK**.

3.   The document is now divided into two sections, although nothing visible seems to have occurred.

☞ **Learn More:** After inserting the section break on the page, the area above the blinking cursor is considered to be "Section 1" and the area below the cursor is now "Section 2."

4.   Go to **Tools > Protect Document.**

5.   The "Protect Document" dialog box appears. In the area labeled "Protect Document For," click inside the circle next to **Forms,** then click on the **Sections** button.

✔**Troubleshooting Tip:** In the event that the **Sections** button is still grayed out after clicking inside the circle next to **Forms**, redo step 2 in this section.

6.   When the "Section Protection" dialog box appears, make sure there is a check next to "Section 1" under "Protected Sections" by clicking inside the small box. The small box to the left of "Section 2" should be empty.

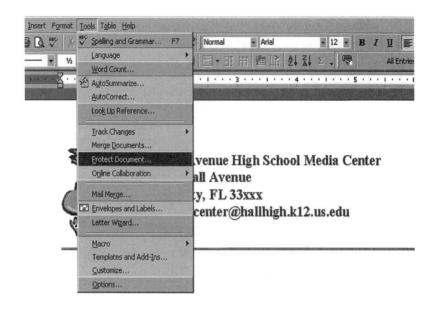

Figure 3.16   Tools Menu

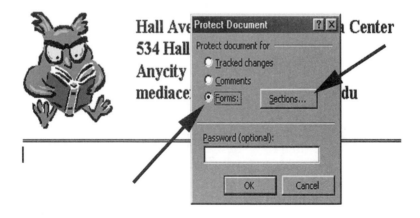

Figure 3.17   "Protect Document" Dialog Box

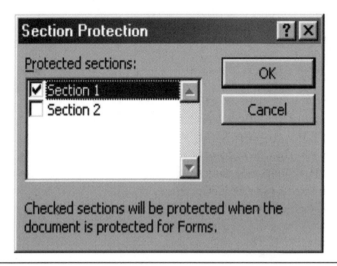

Figure 3.18 "Section Protection" Dialog Box

7. Click on **OK**. The "Section Protection" dialog box is now gone, but the "Protect Document" dialog box is still visible.

8. Inside the box under "Password," enter a password you can easily remember. The actual password is not seen when it is entered; instead, asterisks or black dots appear in place of each letter, numeral, or special character. For this example, enter "My Letter," then press **OK**.

✔ **Troubleshooting Tip:** Passwords are case sensitive. Also, a forgotten password results in not being able to access the stationery to make modifications to it.

☞ **Learn More:** Entering a password inside the box under "Password" is optional. If no password is entered, the protected area is protected from accidental changes, but intentional changes can be made to the protected area by going to the **Menubar** and clicking on **Tools > Unprotect Document** to unprotect the document before making the changes.

9. The "Confirm Password" dialog box appears. Re-enter the same password that was entered on the "Protect Document" dialog box and click **OK**.

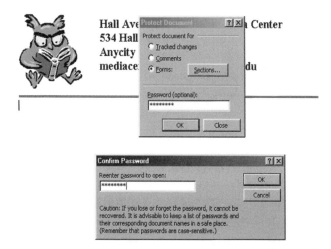

Figure 3.19   Protecting a Document With a Password

All dialog boxes are now gone, and only the stationery is visible.

At this point, the top part of the stationery, which contains the graphic and the address, is protected. Although a person may be able to click inside that area, no changes can be made unless a password has been designated and used to unprotect the document.

 Learn More: To make modifications to a document that has been password protected, go to **Tools > Unprotect Document**. The "Unprotect Document" dialog box appears. Inside the box under "Password," enter the password that was used to protect the document. Click on the **OK** button. The document can now be modified as needed.

Saving a Letterhead as a Template

It is now time to save the stationery as a template.

1. Click **File > Save As.**

2. When the "Save As" dialog box appears, go to the window to the right of "Save As Type" (**MAC**: "Format") located toward the bottom of the dialog box. Click on the arrow on the right side of the box, then click on **Document Template.**

3. In the "Save In" section of the dialog box, "Templates" or "My Templates" should appear. Name the template "Hall Avenue High School Media Center.dot" in the window to the right of "File Name." (**MAC:** Use the same name except for **"Center.dot."**)

✔ **Troubleshooting Tip:** If **Templates** does not appear inside the box to the right of "Save In," locate the "Templates" folder that is part of Microsoft Word. (**MAC 01:** "My Templates" folder is located in the "Templates" folder in Microsoft Office 2001.)

4. Click the **Save** button. The stationery is now saved as a template.

Figure 3.20   Saving the Document as a Template

Accessing a Letterhead Template

1. To access the stationery at some future time, click on **File > New** and select the **General** tab in the "New" dialog box. (**MAC 01: File > Project Gallery**, select "My Templates" from the left column.)

2. Click on the **Hall Avenue High** icon, and the stationery appears.

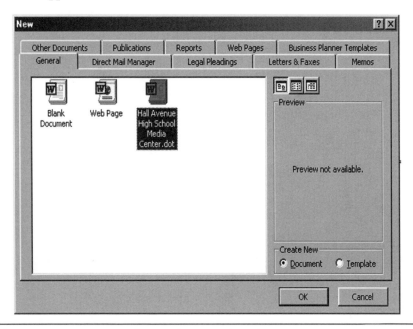

Figure 3.21 Accessing the Newly Created Stationery

Quick Review

Word can be used to create special-purpose stationery. The following is a review of the commands that were covered in this chapter:

► **Change Margins:**

File > Page Setup > Margins tab

► **Locate Clip Art:**

Insert > Picture > Clip Art

► **Resize Clip Art:**

Click on the small box in lower right corner of the selected graphic and drag diagonally toward the center of the graphic to make the graphic smaller or diagonally away from the graphic to make the graphic larger

▶ **Insert a Text Box:**

Drawing Toolbar > Text Box button

▶ **Make a Text Box Border Invisible:**

Double-click on border > Format Text dialog box > Colors and Lines tab > Line area > Color > No Line

▶ **Insert a Line:**

Drawing Toolbar > Line button > Position cursor, hold mouse button down, and drag line to desired length

▶ **Change Line Style:**

Drawing Toolbar > Line Style button

▶ **Insert Section Breaks:**

Insert > Breaks

▶ **Protect a Document:**

Tools > Protect Document > Forms > Sections

▶ **Create a Template:**

File > Save As > Save In > Template

4

Letter Wizard

*O*ne task that can certainly be done in Microsoft Word is to write a letter, and Microsoft Word has developed a "Wizard" that can assist individuals, especially students, in making professional-looking letters. This chapter demonstrates the use of the "Letter Wizard."

1. Once in Microsoft Word, access the "Letter Wizard" by clicking **File,** then **New** to bring up the "New" dialog box.

   MAC 01: **File > Project Gallery**. The "Project Gallery" dialog box will appear. (See Figure 4.1.)

✔ **Troubleshooting Tip**: The **New Blank Document** button does not bring up the "New" Dialog box.

2. Select the **Letters** or **Letters and Faxes** tab and double-click on the **Letter Wizard** or **LETTER.WIZ.**

   MAC 01: Select the **Letters-Envelopes** category and then double-click on **Letter Wizard** in the main window. (See Figure 4.2.)

3. If the "Office Assistant" appears asking for selection of "Send one letter" or "Send letters to a mailing list," choose "Send one letter."

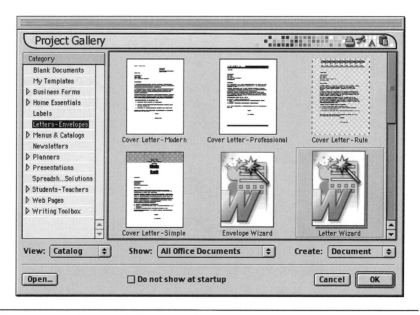

Figure 4.1 Macintosh Project Gallery

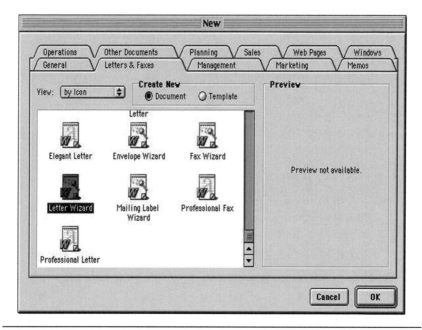

Figure 4.2 Selecting "Letter Wizard" in the "New" Dialog Box

4. The first of four "Letter Wizard" screens emerge. Select the box to the left of the "Date line" if it is not selected. The "Date line" contains the current date. Click on the arrow next to the "Date line" to choose a date format other than the one that appears. For this exercise, select the date format that has the month spelled out followed by the day and year (e.g., May 24, 2001). If no date is desired on the letter, simply click the box next to the "Date" line to make the check mark disappears. No date will be added to the letter.

5. Click on the arrow under "Choose a page design" to view design options. As a particular design is selected, a miniature image of the page design may appear below the name of the design. For this example, "Contemporary" is the selected page design. If "Contemporary" does not appear, choose "Letter-Professional" in the drop-down menu.

6. Move to the "Choose a Letter Style" area. If the current choice is not desired, click on the "down" arrow and choose another letter style. Each time a letter style is selected, a miniature of the letter style appears below the name of the selected style. In the example, a "Semi-Block" page design is used. With this particular design, the date, complimentary closing, and name of the sender all appear toward the right margin, and the first line of each paragraph is indented.

Learn More: The "Modified Block" page design is similar to the "Semi-Block" page design in that the date, complimentary closing, and the name of the sender are all toward the right margin of the letter. However, the first line of each paragraph is not indented. "Full Block" page design means that all elements of the letter are left-justified on the page.

7. Once the letter style decisions are made, click on the **Next** button. (See Figures 4.3 and 4.4.)

8. The "Step 2" dialog box of the "Letter Wizard" is next. On this dialog box, there are places for the "Recipient's" name, address, and a salutation. When the information is filled in, click on the **Next** button.

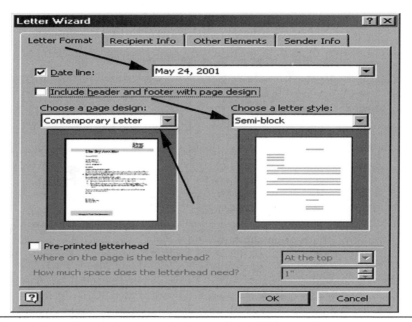

Figure 4.3   Formatting Letter in Letter Wizard (Windows)

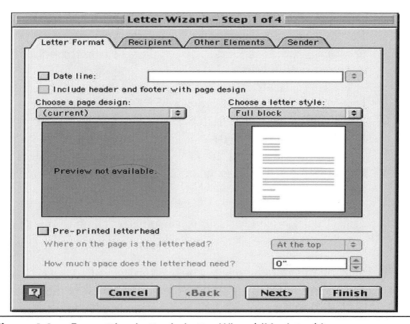

Figure 4.4   Formatting Letter in Letter Wizard (Macintosh)

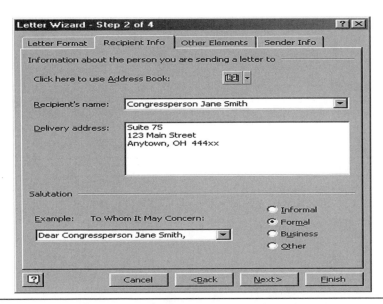

Figure 4.5 Inserting "Recipient" Information into letter

9. In the "Step 3" dialog box of the "Letter Wizard," additional items may be added to the letter. To choose an additional item, click inside the box to the left of the desired item. Once a box is checked, the box to the right of the item becomes active. To select the current contents of the box, do nothing. However, if something different is desired, either click on the "down" arrow to make another choice or type in the desired wording. After the desired choices are made, click on **Next**. (See Figure 4.6.)

10. The "Step 4" dialog box is the final part of the "Letter Wizard." Enter the appropriate information in the box for the "Sender's" name. If inclusion of a return address is desired, type that information in the box to the right of "Return Address." In the event that no return address is to be included in the letter, click inside the box to the left of "Omit," which is below "Return Address." The return address, if included, appears at the bottom of the letter.

11. Selection of a closing is needed. In the "Closing" section, select the arrow next to "Complimentary Closing," then click on the desired closing. After a choice is made, click on **Finish**. (See Figure 4.7.)

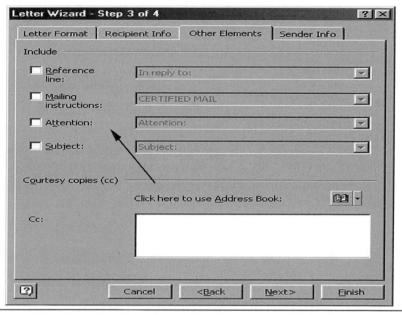

Figure 4.6 Selecting Other Letter Elements in Letter Wizard

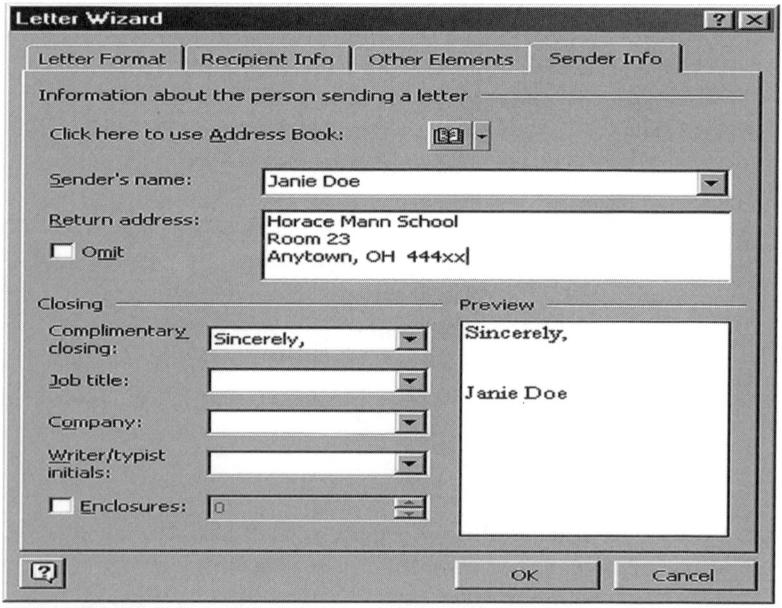

Figure 4.7 Inserting "Sender" Information into Letter Wizard

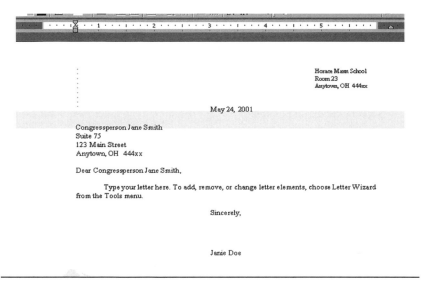

Figure 4.8 Letter on Completion of Letter Wizard,
Before Adding Body of Letter

12. The body of the letter is ready to be entered. To change various "Letter Wizard" elements, go to the **Menubar** and click on **Tools > Letter Wizard**. The "Letter Wizard" comes into view, and the desired changes may be made by going to the appropriate step.

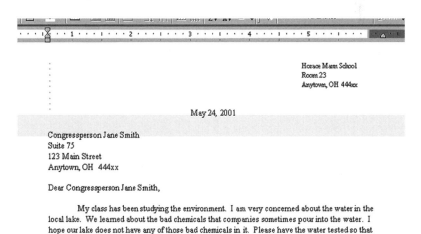

Figure 4.9 Example of Completed Letter

Quick Review

This chapter focused on the use of the "Letter Wizard." As part of this chapter, the following commands were covered:

▶ **Open Letter Wizard:**

File > New > Letters and Faxes tab > Letter Wizard and Create New > Document > OK

WIN 97:   File > New > Letters tab > LETTER.WIZ

MAC 01:   File > Project Gallery > Letters-Envelopes > Letter Wizard

▶ **Letter Wizard Steps:**

Specify single or multiple letters: "Office Assistant" > "Send one letter" or "Send letters to a mailing list"

Step 1 dialog box > "Date" line, "Choose Page Design," and "Choose A Letter Style" > Next

Step 2 dialog box > "Recipient's" name, address, and salutation > Next

Step 3 dialog box > "Reference" line, "Mailing" instructions, "Attention," "Subject," and "Courtesy" copies > Next

Step 4 dialog box > "Sender's" name, return address, and closing > Finish > Enter body of letter

▶ **Make Changes to Letter:**

Tools > Letter Wizard

W 5

Creating a Certificate

Rather than going to a local teachers' supply store to purchase commercially produced certificates, personalized certificates can easily be made using Microsoft Word. This exercise shows how to make a certificate, how to change page orientation, and how to use page borders and "WordArt." Font characteristics are also covered in this chapter.

Changing the Page Orientation

When creating a certificate, the best layout is "Landscape Orientation." This simply means that the paper is horizontal in nature. The normal layout for letters and documents is "Portrait," which means the paper is vertical.

1. With a blank Microsoft Word document open, go to the **Menu-bar** and select **File > Page Setup.**

   MAC: **Format > Document**

2. A dialog box appears. Click on the **Margins** tab.

3. By each of the margins (top, bottom, left, and right), "up" and "down" arrows are located to the right of the box that contains the current margin settings. If different margin settings are

desired, click the appropriate arrow next to the margins until the desired margins appear. In the example, each margin is set to **0.5"**.

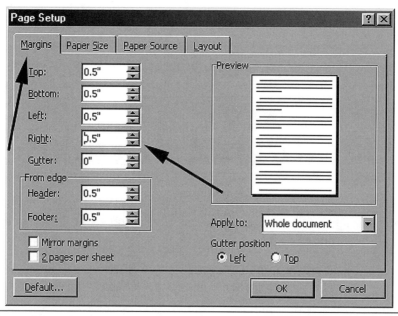

Figure 5.1   Setting Document Margins (Windows)

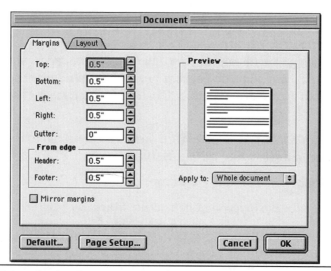

Figure 5.2   Setting Document Margins (Macintosh)

4. Click the **Paper Size** tab.

5. In the **Orientation** section, there are two choices: **Portrait** and **Landscape**. Select "Landscape." (**MAC:** The second button after "Orientation" is "Landscape.") A miniature of the page appears in the "Preview" section of the dialog box. Click **OK**.

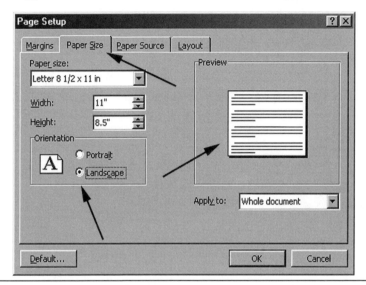

Figure 5.3 Selecting Landscape Page Orientation (Windows)

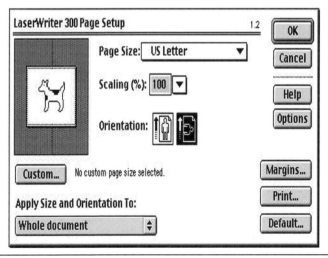

Figure 5.4 Selecting Landscape Page Orientation (Macintosh)

Adding a Border

1. At this point, the paper has a horizontal orientation. Hit **Enter/ Return** 10 times.

2. Go to the **Menubar** and select **Format > Borders and Shading (Mac 2001: Format > Border)**.

3. The "Borders and Shading" dialog box appears. Click on the **Page Border** tab.

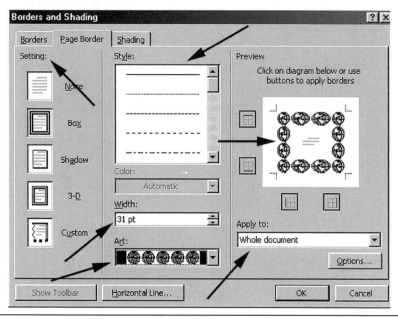

Figure 5.5   Adding a Page Border

4. In the "Setting" section, choose the desired type of border. In the example, the "Box" setting is used for the border.

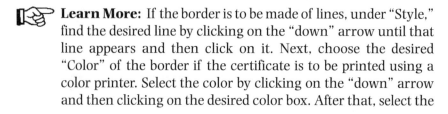 **Learn More:** If the border is to be made of lines, under "Style," find the desired line by clicking on the "down" arrow until that line appears and then click on it. Next, choose the desired "Color" of the border if the certificate is to be printed using a color printer. Select the color by clicking on the "down" arrow and then clicking on the desired color box. After that, select the

desired line width by clicking on the "down" arrow under "Width" until the desired width appears and then click on it.

5. In the event that artwork is to be used to create the border of the certificate, disregard the "Style" and "Color" sections. Instead, under **Art**, choose the desired artwork by clicking on the "down" arrow until the desired artwork comes into view and then click on it. Selection of the desired width of the artwork is made as described above. In the example, artwork with a 31-pt. width is used for the border (made up of globes).

6. A miniature version of the certificate border appears in the "Preview" section. In the "Apply To" section, which is under the "Preview" section, make sure "Whole Document" is selected.

7. Click on **OK**. The dialog box disappears, and the selected border appears on all four sides of the page.

Adding WordArt

1. Adding **WordArt** is the next step in creating a certificate. If the **WordArt** button is not visible, go to the **Menu Bar** and click on **View > Toolbars > WordArt**.

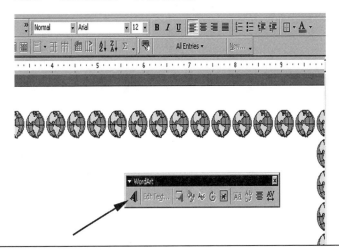

Figure 5.6   WordArt Button on WordArt Toolbar

✔ **Troubleshooting Tip:** The **WordArt** button can also be found on the **Drawing Toolbar,** which can be accessed by going to **View > Toolbars > Drawing.**

2. Click on the **WordArt** button, and the "WordArt Gallery" dialog box appears.

3. Select a **WordArt Style** by clicking on the desired style. In the example, the WordArt style selected is the third one in the first row.

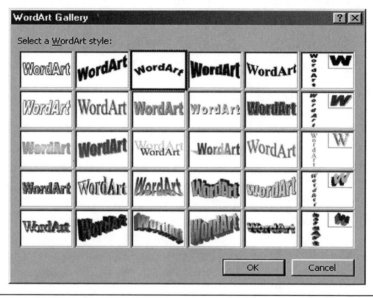

Figure 5.7 WordArt Gallery

4. Click **OK** and the "Edit WordArt Text" dialog box appears.

Modifying WordArt

1. Under "Font," the current font appears. If the font given is not the desired font, click the "down" arrow and select another font. "Arial Black" is the font used in the example.

 Learn More: Any text that is placed on a page needs to be easily read. The fancier the font or WordArt, the more difficult it is to read. When possible, select somewhat plain text or WordArt.

2. The words "Your Text Here" appear in the large white box. Those words are highlighted, so simply enter "Good Citizen Award."

3. Under "Size," change the font size to 60.

4. Click on the **B** button to make the text bold. For our example, we will leave the italics off and click **OK.**

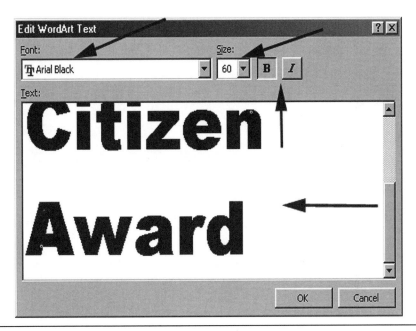

Figure 5.8   Editing WordArt Text

5. The WordArt now appears on the certificate. Move the WordArt to the top of the page as seen in the example. Place the cursor on top of the WordArt until it changes into a "plus" sign with arrows at each end (or a hand in **Mac 2001**). While holding the mouse button down, drag the WordArt to the top of the page.

Troubleshooting Tip: If the WordArt appears too large for the page, it can easily be modified by double-clicking on the WordArt. (Do not click on the WordArt button that appears on the toolbar.) At that point, the "Edit WordArt Text" dialog box emerges, and changes can also be made to the wording and font.

Figure 5.9   Certificate with WordArt

👉 **Learn More:** After a WordArt style has been selected, a different shape may be desired. To alter the shape of the WordArt, single-click on the WordArt so that the eight tiny boxes appear around the WordArt; then, click on the **WordArt Shape** button on the **WordArt Toolbar.** A menu of 30 shapes appears. Click on the desired one, and the WordArt on the page changes to that newly selected shape.

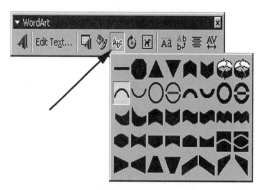

Figure 5.10   Changing a WordArt Shape

Learn More: In the event that a change to another WordArt style is desired, single-click on the WordArt so that the eight tiny boxes appear around the WordArt. Single-click the **WordArt Gallery** button on the **WordArt Toolbar.** When the WordArt Gallery appears, single click on the desired WordArt style and then click on the **OK** button. The original WordArt style changes to the newly selected style.

6. If a different color is desired for the WordArt, click on the **Format WordArt** button on the "WordArt" toolbar.

 Learn More: If the certificate is going to be printed in black and white, using black for the WordArt color provides the best results.

7. The "Format WordArt" dialog box comes into view. Click on the "down" arrow next to the color box to the right of the **Fill-Color** option.

8. When the color palette pops down, click on **Fill Effects**.

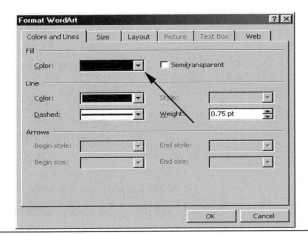

Figure 5.11 Fill-Color Option on the Format WordArt Dialog Box

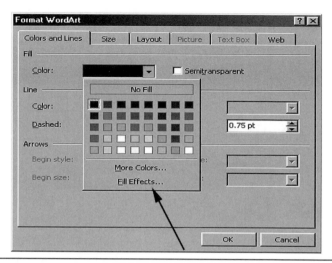

Figure 5.12 Fill Effects Button

9. The "Fill Effects" dialog box is now visible. For this example, click in the circle next to "Two Colors" in the "Color" section.

10. To choose the first color, click the "down" arrow next to the color box under "Color 1." Select the color green for this example. Next, choose the second color by clicking on the "down" arrow next to the color box under "Color 2." Select the color teal.

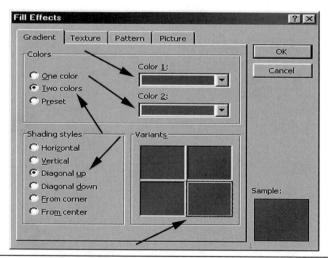

Figure 5.13 Fill Effects Gradient Choices

11. Select "Diagonal Up" in the **Shading Styles** section of the "Fill Effects" dialog box. In our example, we selected the fourth variant.

12. Click **OK** to exit the "Fill Effects" dialog box and then click **OK** to exit the "Format WordArt" dialog box.

Adding Text

1. Additional text is now ready to be added to the certificate. Click toward the bottom of the page and then select the **Center Alignment** button on the toolbar. The cursor should be blinking in the middle of the screen.

 Troubleshooting Tip: If the **Center Alignment** button is not visible, go to the **Menubar**, and click on **View > Toolbars > Formatting**.

Learn More: There are four alignment buttons in Microsoft Word. To the left of the **Center Alignment** button is the **Left Alignment** button. Immediately to the right of the **Center Alignment** button is the **Right Alignment** button. The fourth  alignment button is the **Justify** button, which causes the line(s) of text to be aligned along both the left *and* right margins.

 Troubleshooting Tip: If the desired font for the certificate does not appear in the font box, click on the "down" arrow and then locate and click on the desired font. In the example, "Arial" is the selected font.

2. If the desired font size for the does not appear in the "Font Size" box, click on the "down" arrow and then locate and click on the desired font size. In the example, the selected font size is 18 pt. for most of the body of the certificate.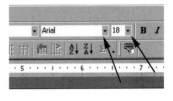

Learn More: In the event that a font color other than the current color (probably black) is desired for the text contained in the body of the certificate, single-click on the "down" arrow to the right of the Font Color button on the toolbar to make a font color palette appear. 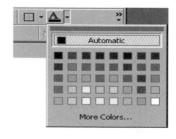 Click on a color to select it. Typed text now appears in the new color.

3. Type "This is presented to" in font size 18 pt. and press **Enter/Return** three times.

4. Change the font size to a larger size. In the example, a 26-pt. font size is used.

5. Click on the **B** button on the toolbar so the print appears in bold font style.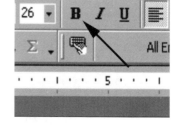

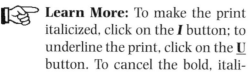 **Learn More:** To make the print italicized, click on the *I* button; to underline the print, click on the <u>U</u> button. To cancel the bold, italicized, or underline font style, click on the associated button.

6. Type the recipient's name and press **Enter/Return** three times.

7. Select a font size smaller than the one used for the recipient's name. Again, in the example, an 18-pt. font size is used.

8. Type the body of the certificate. At the end of each line of print in the body of the certificate, press **Enter/Return**.

9. Press **Enter/Return** seven times. The number of times the **Enter/Return** key is pressed varies according to the amount of wording in the body of the certificate and font size.

10. Type the name of the person awarding the certificate.

11. Press the **Tab** key on the computer's keyboard nine times and type the date the certificate is to be awarded. The number of

times the **Tab** key is pressed varies according to length of the name and size of the font.

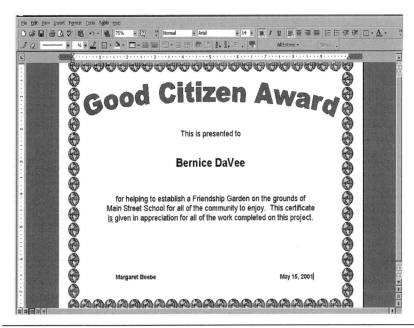

Figure 5.14   Completed Certificate

12.   The certificate is now ready to be printed and signed.

Figure 5.15   Printed Certificate

Quick Review

▶ **Change margins:**

WIN: File > Page Setup

MAC: Then choose Orientation Margins tab

▶ **Change Page Orientation:**

WIN: File > Page Setup > Paper Size tab > select Portrait or Landscape

MAC: File > Page Setup > Orientations > Paper Size tab > select Portrait or Landscape

▶ **Adding Shading and Borders:**

Format > Borders and Shading or Borders > Page Border tab

▶ **Adding WordArt:**

Select **WordArt button**

View > Toolbars > WordArt

View > Toolbars > Drawing

▶ **Modify WordArt:**

Click on the WordArt to bring up the WordArt dialog box and change the text, font style, or font size.

Double-click on WordArt to bring up the WordArt Toolbar. Click on the Word Shape button to change the overall shape or the Format WordArt button for many more options.

6

Readability Analysis

One of the features in Microsoft Word is a handy tool for assisting teachers in determining the reading level of text: the reading statistics feature. One component of determining the readability level of printed material is an examination of the text for aspects such as the number of words, number of sentences, and number of paragraphs. Microsoft Word uses the Flesch-Kincaid readability formula, which examines text to determine the reading level of the text; the level is reported in terms of grade level. Once a grade level for text is determined, students reading at or above the determined level should have few, if any, problems understanding the text. Thus, before using a piece of literature in a classroom, it may be desirable to check the readability level of the material to determine, by typing a short sample of the text into Microsoft Word, whether the material is appropriate for the reading level of the students.

To conduct a readability analysis on a passage of text, make sure that Microsoft Word is set up to perform the analysis. Before starting the steps below, open a blank document in Microsoft Word.

1. Go to the **Menubar** and click on **Tools > Options.**

    MAC 98:   **Tools > Preferences**

    MAC 01:   **Edit > Preferences**

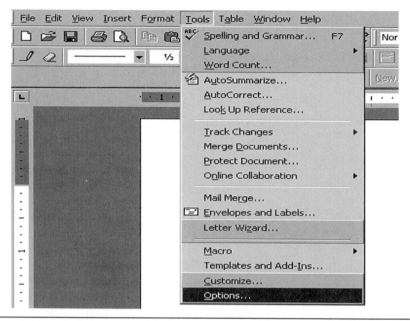

Figure 6.1   Tools Menu

2. At this point, the "Options" dialog box appears. Click on the **Spelling** or **Spelling and Grammar** tab. The last item in the "Grammar" section reads, "Show readability statistics." Click the box to the left of that item to checkmark it. Click on **OK**. (See Figure 6.2.)

3. To obtain an approximate reading level of the chosen textbook material, type in a passage that is at least 100 words in length. This is the same length used by some popular readability formulas. If you are checking the readability of an entire book, select a minimum of one 100-word passage from the front of the book, one 100-word passage from the middle of the book, and a third 100-word passage from the end of the book, and do a readability analysis on each of the passages. Type the appropriate text passage(s) into an open Microsoft Word document. The example in Box 6.1, two stanzas from "The Raven" by Edgar Allan Poe, could be used to check for reading level. (See Box 6.1.)

4. Go to the **Menubar** and click on **Tools > Spelling and Grammar**.

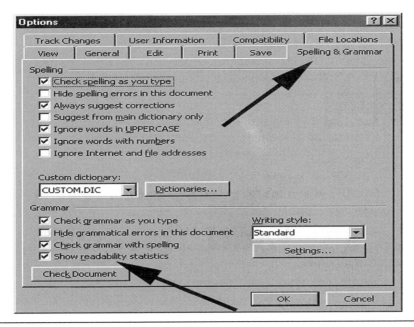

Figure 6.2   "Options" Dialog Box

BOX 6.1
Readability Sample Passage

Once upon a midnight dreary, while I pondered, weak and weary,
Over many a quaint and curious volume of forgotten lore,
While I nodded, nearly napping, suddenly there came a tapping,
As of some one gently rapping, rapping at my chamber door.
"'Tis some visitor," I muttered, "tapping at my chamber door—
Only this and nothing more."

Ah, distinctly I remember it was in the bleak December,
And each separate dying ember wrought its ghost upon the floor.
Eagerly I wished the morrow;—vainly I had sought to borrow
From my books surcease of sorrow—sorrow for the lost Lenore—
For the rare and radiant maiden whom the angels name
Lenore—

SOURCE: Edgar Allan Poe, "The Raven," first published in 1845. Retrieved 2/27/01 from The Raven Society of the University of Virginia: www. student.Virginia.edu/~ravens/raven.html

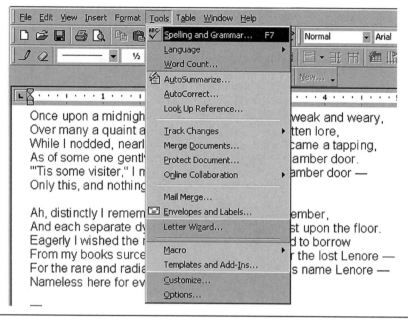

Figure 6.3 Performing the Spelling and Grammar Check

5. After the spelling and grammar check are complete, the "Readability Statistics" dialog box appears. The last item gives the calculated grade level for the text passage entered. This assists in determining whether the reading level of the material is appropriate for particular students. (See Figure 6.4.)

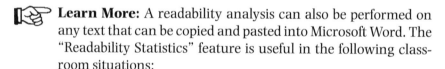 **Learn More:** A readability analysis can also be performed on any text that can be copied and pasted into Microsoft Word. The "Readability Statistics" feature is useful in the following classroom situations:

▶ Conducting a readability analysis on a textbook that is under consideration for adoption.

▶ After older students write stories for younger children, the students can conduct a readability-level analysis on the stories to see whether the reading level is appropriate for the younger age group. The students can do this while checking their stories for spelling and grammar errors.

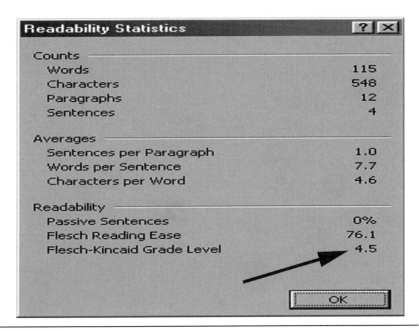

Figure 6.4   "Readability Statistics" Dialog Box

▶ Before having students visit a particular Web site, determine whether the reading level of the site is appropriate for them. To do this, highlight the text on the Web site, copy the text, paste the text into a new Microsoft Word document, and then perform the spelling and grammar check to obtain the readability statistics.

Quick Review

Performing a readability analysis on a passage of text is as easy as conducting a spelling and grammar check. The most time-consuming part is entering the text into the document so that an analysis can be done. Following the steps below completes a readability analysis:

▶ **Readability Analysis Setup:**

Blank Document > Tools > Options > "Options" dialog box > Spelling and Grammar tab > "Grammar" section > Show "Readability Statistics" > OK

► **Enter Text:**

Enter or Copy and Paste an approximately 100-word passage into the blank document

► **Conduct Readability Analysis:**

Tools > Spelling and Grammar

7

Making Web Pages

A file created to be a Web page uses "hypertext markup language," also called "HTML." Microsoft Word makes simple HTML files (Web pages) that can be used on the Internet. However, Word cannot be used to make complex Web pages. Microsoft Word is a full-featured word processing program, whereas Microsoft FrontPage is a full-featured program designed to make Web pages only. Word has incorporated several different ways to create a Web page, and this chapter describes three: converting a file, opening a new file as a Web page, using "Sample Web Pages," and an introduction to the "Web Page Wizard."

One easy way to make a Web page is to simply save an existing document as a Web page. This will "convert" the file from the word processor format (document) into the HTML format. You have previously created documents entitled "Lesson Plan," first as a regular file and again as a document template. We will open the "Lesson Plan" word processing file and "convert" it to a Web page.

Converting a Word Document

1. Click on the **Open** icon and navigate to your lesson plan document. (Hint: **Windows** users may have saved it in "My Documents." **Macintosh** users may have saved it in the Macintosh HD.) The screen will show the lesson plan.

2. Go to **File > Save As Web Page**

WIN 97 & MAC 98: File > Save As HTML

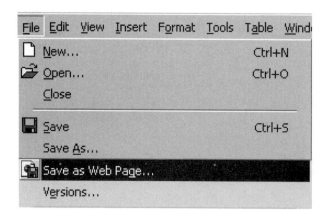

Figure 7.1 Save as Web Page

Troubleshooting Tip: If the **Save As HTML** or **Save As Web Page** options are not found in the File Menu, choose **Save As** and select "HTML Documents" or "Web Page" in the bottom "File Type" or "Format" window.

3. Word will suggest using the file name "Lesson Plan." However, to be used by both Netscape Navigator and Internet Explorer, Web pages must have file names with no spaces.

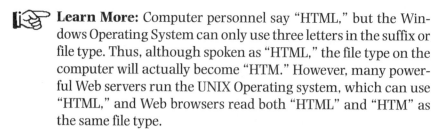 **Learn More:** Computer personnel say "HTML," but the Windows Operating System can only use three letters in the suffix or file type. Thus, although spoken as "HTML," the file type on the computer will actually become "HTM." However, many powerful Web servers run the UNIX Operating system, which can use "HTML," and Web browsers read both "HTML" and "HTM" as the same file type.

Do NOT use the name "Lesson Plan" for an HTML file. It must be titled "lessonplan," and more specifically, it would be "lessonplan.htm." Change the file name as shown and also note that the file type or format window displayed at the very bottom of the dialog box should say "HTML Document" or "Web Page."

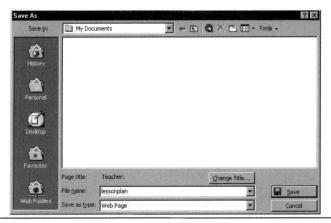

Figure 7.2 "Save As Web Page" Dialog Box

4. Once the "Lesson Plan" has been saved as a Web page, you are finished. You've created a simple Web page simply through a "Save As" feature in Microsoft Word.

 Learn More: To use Web pages on the Internet, you would normally place them onto a computer Web server. However, you may easily "test" your Web page "lessonplan.htm" by opening it with any Web browser. If you start up either Netscape Navigator or Internet Explorer, the browser can "see" the file and open your new Web page. Note that a Web browser will NOT open a word processing file.

Web pages that have been converted can easily be edited in Word. The appearance of the file does not show any difference, but there is a change to the toolbar. The farthest left icon will show a dot on the "page" when a Web page is in the active window, as in the "Web Toolbar Changes" figure. (**Word 97:** The toolbar automatically changes to different options.) You may use the editing features in Word to make a more attractive Web page, such as adding a background color and changing font sizes. Word can also add graphic images, but that operation is beyond the scope of this book.

MAC 98: There is no visible difference between a document file and a Web page.

MAC 01: The icon in the border on the top of the active window will appear differently for a Web page than for a document.

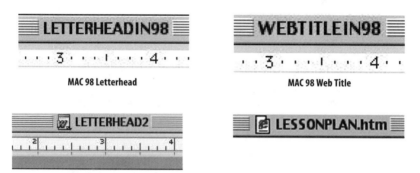

MAC 98 Letterhead

MAC 98 Web Title

MAC 2001 Letterhead

MAC 2001 Web Title

Opening a New File as a Web Page

You will be creating an informational Web page for the "Hall Avenue High School Media Center." Opening a blank Web page is very simple because a template is available.

1. **File > New > Web Pages > Blank Web Page > OK** and leave the file blank for now.

   MAC 01: **File > Project Gallery > Web Page > OK**

   WIN 00: **File > New > Web Page > OK**

2. Click the **Open** icon and navigate to the "Hall Avenue High" document template created in Chapter 3. Make sure "Document Templates" is selected in the "File Type" or "Format" window at the very bottom of the "Open" dialog box.

   MAC 01: In the "Show" window, select "Word Templates."

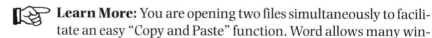 **Learn More:** You are opening two files simultaneously to facilitate an easy "Copy and Paste" function. Word allows many win-

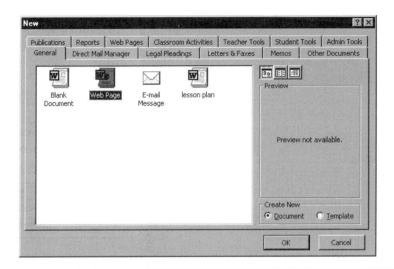

Figure 7.2 "Open New Web Page" Dialog Box

dows to be opened at once, with additional options as to how they can be displayed on your screen.

3. Recall that this is a "protected" document. We will temporarily remove the protection. Go to **Tools > Unprotect Document**. Type in your password. (Hint: "My Letter" was the suggested password in Chapter 3.)

4. Highlight and copy all of the text information, which is inside a "text box," but do not copy the graphic. After you have copied the text, "protect" the file and close the stationery template.

5. Switch from "Hall Avenue" to the blank Web page by **Window > Document #** (you should only have two items from which to choose).

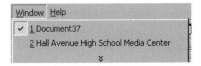

6. Now, paste in the information copied from the letterhead by using the **Paste icon** on the toolbar. The basic address information will now be in the new Web page.

☞ **Learn More:** Note that the functions of "Cut" and "Copy" are grayed out, indicating that they cannot be used at this time. They are only highlighted when something is selected.

7. Highlight the text and tap **Center Alignment.** Click at the end of the text to deselect it.

8. Press **Enter/Return twice.** The e-mail address will be underlined, which indicates that Word has automatically inserted a "hyperlink." The **@** tells Word that this line is a username.

9. Skip one line, then add "Phone: 123-456-7890." Tap Enter/Return, add "Fax: 123-456-7899." Tap **Enter/Return** twice and then add "Hours of Operation: 8 a.m. to 5 p.m. M-F." The information should now look like this:

Hall Avenue High School Media Center
534 Hall Avenue
Anycity, FL 33xxx

mediacenter@hallhigh.k12.us.edu

Phone: 123-456-7890
Fax: 123-456-7899

Hours of Operation: 8 a.m. to 5 p.m. M-F

☞ **Learn More:** A "hyperlink," or "link," in a Web page causes an action, often moving to a different selection of information or to an entirely different location on the Internet. In this case, the "link" will automatically "start" a user's electronic mail program (when configured) when they click on the link.

10. The Web page should now be saved. Again, Word will suggest the long file name, "Hall Avenue High . . .," but Web page file

names cannot have any spaces. Thus, change the name to **hallmediacenter.htm.**

You now have an example of a Web page that could be used to supply basic information, and it has a "link" to start an electronic mail program. The e-mail address is also clearly visible for those who may use a different type of electronic mail program.

 Learn More: Feel free to experiment with different type sizes, colors, and other features creating Web pages in Word. Be aware that you can create a file that appears to be correct in Word but may not display properly in Netscape or Internet Explorer, which is how they would look "on the Web." You should always check Web page files in a browser before you try to use the files on a Web server.

Sample Web Pages and Web Page Wizards

Microsoft Word has included both "Web Page Wizards" and "Sample Web Pages" to assist teachers in creating Web pages one step at a time. The "Wizards" that Microsoft has developed for Word are significantly different in each version of Word. In fact, the Macintosh 98 version of Word uses the term "Wizard," as does Windows 97 and 2000; however, the Macintosh 2001 version provides a number of Web page samples in the "Project Gallery." Thus, we will provide an introduction only to the concept of using Wizards or Sample Web Pages.

Introduction to Using Sample Web Pages

Word offers several "sample" versions of Web pages. These are found under **File > New > Web Pages.** The samples are "mock-up" Web pages. They typically include the layout, headings, and sample data. They are designed so that the user can replace the information with their own and add additional elements as desired. After "customizing" the sample, the user can change the title before saving the Web page. Note that most sample pages will create a single Web page file. A sample from Windows 2000 is shown below.

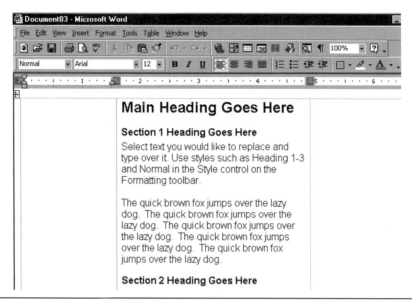

Figure 7.3   Sample Web Page

MAC 01:   The "Project Gallery" includes blank documents and templates. Under the category "Web Pages,"

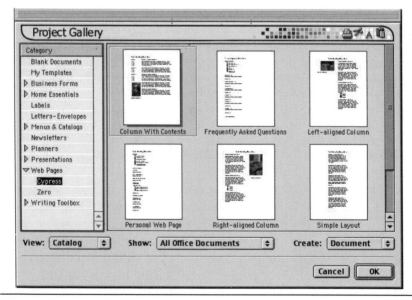

Figure 7.4   Sample Web Page

Word offers several selections, including "Personal Web Page" and "Sample Web Page."

✔ **Troubleshooting Tip:** If your computer does not have the Sample Web Pages or Wizards being showcased in this section, they can be located on the Microsoft Office installation CD.

Introduction to Web Page Wizard

As you found in using Letter Wizards in Chapter 4, a Wizard uses step-by-step instructions and "fill in the blank" fields to help you create a personalized document. They are designed to make complex document creation easy by supplying a prespecified "design." In the case of creating a Web page, the Wizard asks questions concerning "navigation" and "file location" that are more involved than simply making a single file. When you can supply the information, the Web Page Wizard is very useful.

The Web pages made with "Sample Web Pages" typically result in a single "page." However, any Web page that uses both text and a single graphic would result in two separate files. One would be the "HTML" file described previously, plus the graphic that would typically be either a "JPEG" or "GIF" file. The Web Page Wizard creates multiple pages, and it is beyond the scope of this book to fully explain file locations, graphic files, and other features of Web pages to fully use a Wizard. However, you are encouraged to experiment with using the Wizards, which can make more complex Web pages than the Sample Web Pages.

 Learn More: Microsoft Word and Microsoft FrontPage, though separate programs, are closely linked.

Quick Review

▶ **A Web page is also called an "HTML" file.**

▶ **Word offers several methods of making Web pages:**

1. Converting a document: File > Save as Web Page or HTML

2. Opening a new Web page

   WIN 97 & MAC 98:   File > New > Web Pages >
   Blank Web Page

   WIN 2000:   File > New > Web Page

   MAC 2001:   File > Project Gallery > Web Page

3. Using Web Page Wizards: File>New>Web Pages tab > Web
   Page Wizard

▶ **Web pages can be opened in either Netscape Navigator
or Internet Explorer.**

▶ **Multitasking:**

Word can easily open two or more files simultaneously. After
opening multiple Word files, view them and arrange them in
the Window menu.

▶ **Sample Web Pages:**

"Mock-up" pages allow you to replace the sample information
with your own but keep any styles, color, and so on.

▶ **Web Page Wizards:**

Web Page Wizards allow you to insert personalized information into a "template-like" format. They typically consist of
multiple "pages."

Index

**CORWIN
PRESS**

The Corwin Press logo—a raven striding across an open book—represents the happy union of courage and learning. We are a professional-level publisher of books and journals for K-12 educators, and we are committed to creating and providing resources that embody these qualities. Corwin's motto is "Success for All Learners."